DAN BILZERIAN:
RICH AND
THICK WITH
CHICKS

— ᛭ —

A BIOGRAPHY OF A MODERN DAY
PLAYBOY.

NATE PLISSKEN

1st edition Copyright © 2020 by Nate Plissken.

2nd edition Copyright @2022 by Nate Plissken.

ISBN: 9798832404769

Trigger warning, this book contains strong language and topics of sexuality that some people may find offensive. Although we do not intend to be offensive, but have endeavoured to keep the content 100% accurate to the source material. This book does not condone sexual harassment or sexist behavior towards women. This book is intended to be journalistic. We do not draw conclusions about morality and ethics but let the reader make his or her own judgements.

Be warned again if words like: "fuck or pussy or asshole" offend you, then stop reading right now. Also, this is a revised second edition of this book and was designed to give the reader a better quality reading experience than the initial edition. Also, more information has come to light about Dan Bilzerian's life in recent years, and we have made updates based on those facts.

CONTENTS

INTRODUCTION

DAN BILZERIAN
RICH & THICK WITH CHICKS
A Candid Biography of a modern day playboy

NATE PLISSKEN

Dan Bilzerian has been called The King of Instagram, a playboy, a poker star, a gun enthusiast, bodybuilder, a THC fanatic, and a drug user a fraud and a trust fund baby. But who is the real Dan Bilzerian? In Dan's case, reality is stranger than fiction. He's known as the party King. His parties have been some of the craziest of all time. Outspoken about the intentional 30 to 1 ratio of females to males at his parties. Something Dan learned from his college days, to increase the ratio of hot girls to guys. He explains the benefits of this ratio from the perspective of the men.

Dan has made it a point to get women to chase him versus chasing them.

"When a woman is chasing you, and she finally fucks you, it's like she accomplished something," said Bilzerian on a 2021 podcast. "Versus like when you're fucking—like—aggressively hitting on her, chasing her ass around the fucking bar all night and then when she does she's like, oh man, I shouldn't have done that. Or like, you know, when you are hitting on her. She's like looking on all these reasons why your not good enough or why she shouldn't fuck you. Because like, you know, she knows she can have you, right?"

Dan then went onto show a comparison of what it's like for hot girls to be hit on and people who pitch millionaires on a business deals. "Like, if... A guy off the street is pitching you a business deal. The first thing you are thinking about is like, you know, all the reasons why this won't work. You know? well the same thing when you're hitting on a girl, she's thinking of all the reasons why you—like— you're not good enough to fuck her or whatever, all the things wrong with you. Versus if she sees you surrounded by some fucking hot girls. She's curious about you, and she comes up to you and you're kind of like dismissive. Now all of a sudden, it's like You're the same guy. She's the same girl at the same fucking bar. But now she's like, she wants to fuck you... I don't know man—people don't understand like the importance of like, getting a girl to chase you."

He grew up wealthy. His parents raised him in a multi-million dollar mansion, but his father never spent a lot of money on expensive cars or jets to impress the ladies, and that was something Dan wanted to indulge in. And he did!

"What is the point of having FU money if you never say Fuck." - Dan Bilzerian.

A motto that is the opposite of Sir John Templeton's, who said, "It's okay to rich if you don't enjoy it."

Some people would say Dan built Ignite as a lifestyle brand and as an excuse to write off expensive parties and toys to impress the ladies. He hired some of the hottest models to build his brand. He wasn't shy about slapping the Ignite logo on everything, including skimpy string bikinis worn by some of the most attractive women in the world.

Ignite was a way to celebrate excess. Even the product, THC, aka the marijuan business, which would prove populr with the ladies but un-profitable for the company.

"My dad said invest in movies,nascar and buy a plane if you hate money, so I did all 3."–Dan Bilzerian

Everything in Dan's life seemed to be about the image he wanted to craft. Even his luxurious 56 million dollar mansion in Bel Air that everyone thought he owned was being rented at his company Ignites expense for $200,000 a month! But was his strategy not a valid one? He gave his brand Ignite a lot of attention. But in 2020 when his company reported a staggering 50 million dollar loss, Bilzerian claimed he just picked the wrong product. And his argument is sound, actually.

Did Dan tryout for the Navy SEALS just to be able to impress women?

In an interview talking about his SEAL training and two Hell Weeks, Bilzerian mentioned he wasn't really a team player and didn't really want a career as a Navy SEAL. It was more about his image he was trying to craft. Why did he get dropped 2 days before graduation from BUDS?

Has Dan Bilzerian's life been crafted by his desire to live outside the shadow of his father?

Many people know that Dan Bilzerian's father, Paul Bilzerian, went to prison for securities fraud after making multiple millions of dollars. But did you know that Paul Bilzerian was a Vietnam veteran who was awarded a bronze star and made it to the rank of an officer? At least in Dan's early life, his father was absent a lot. Did that motivate Dan to attempt to become a Navy SEAL, to gain the approval of his father, the combat veteran?

How did Dan develop his image or his brand?

I have seen little talk about Dan Bilzerian's style choices he has honed over the years. Interestingly enough, many guys lose touch with style and fashion when they get over 30 but not Dan Bilzerian. His choices are unique to him. Like Steve Jobs, he has a daily uniform of fashion he generally wears. It comprises a high quality white t-shirt and various athletic shorts which colors vary but are a solid color, usually orange or red and white tennis shoes. This repetitive daily dress code gives the impression that Dan doesn't want to think about what to wear from day to day. It could also mean that Dan wants to brand his image a certain way with repetition. But what message is he sending with these fashion choices? Well, he looks like he is always ready to go swimming or to the beach. His fashion choices would actually make him look a like a life guard most of the time. Another possible reason for the white shirt and white shoes, which I learned from a model, is that white makes your skin look darker in comparison. Dan usually has a tan, but not always. Have I missed anything? His manicured beard and his iconic hair style have made his personal brand distinctive. He mentioned before that his hair stylist was also his mushroom dealer. Dan has not been shy about his recreational drug use. According to Dan, it's not a good idea to do shrooms for the first time in a public movie theater, instead go somewhere out in nature.

Speaking of your brand—If you build it, they will come or you will cum.

"Like I always say, never put off till tomorrow, you know, pussy that you can fuck today."–Dan Bilzerian.

One thing Dan has is a hard work ethic for fucking chicks. He said: "I think a million fucking things can happen like, you know, it's like when you've got a girl who's willing to fuck you, like I always say like never put off till tomorrow you know... that you can fuck her today because you fucked her today you can always fuck her tomorrow but if you don't like do her today, you may not you know..."

Let's dive deeper into who is Dan Bilzerian?

CHAPTER 1

When the name Dan Bilzerian pops up, various titles come on the scene; these include words like the Instagram King, Blitz, Instagram's Playboy King, and celebrity poker player. Many people have diverse opinions about this interesting California-based individual. Dan Bilzerian's life extends beyond being a gambler, venture capitalist, and an actor with a net worth of $200 million.

We widely known him across the world today—all thanks to a gigantic following on Twitter, Instagram, and other social media platforms—of which many of us agree on. If I may ask, how did you first get to know about this social media influencer with behemoths of followers? Instagram, Twitter, Facebook, blogs, websites, or the news?

Let's face it... on Instagram alone, Dan Bilzerian had about 30 million followers—this excludes the millions of followers he had on Twitter and Facebook as well. He was often spotted with high-end gun collections, fleets of luxury vehicles, mega-mansions—including his 38,000 square foot Bel Air mega-mansion worth $65 million, and not forgetting the endless groups of hot bikini-clad and sometimes, bare-breasted ladies.

However, above all these luxuries, only a few know the history of this jaunty internet sensation with an Armenian descent. You may have asked yourself at some points who Dan is and what makes him special. There was a time I had this question on my mind as well. Yes, I watched his videos; they are quite spectacular and immersive.

But then I sat down to understand who Dan Bilzerian is underneath the surface of his flamboyant lifestyle, which I will share with you right now. For the record, all that you see on the internet about Dan, or "Danny" like I call him, didn't just pop out of nowhere. It took years of determination and calculated risks for him to realize his long-term dreams. So, let's get right to it. Who is Dan Bilzerian and what do we know about his history?

On December 7, 1980, Daniel Brandon Bilzerian was born in Tampa, Florida, United States, to Paul Alec Bilzerian, an Armenian-American investor, business owner, and corporate takeover specialist; and Terri Steffen—in reality, not much is known about her history or activities.

Paul Bilzerian's character depicts that of a corporate raider. His rise to fame on Wall Street came after migrating to the US, shortly after the Armenian genocide. Speaking of being a corporate raider, the white-bushy-mustachioed Armenian's wealth, part of which made him a Wall Street felon, resulted from him purchasing pump and dump stocks from various companies like Cluett Peabody & Co., Pay 'N Pak Stores Inc., Hammermill Paper Co., Singer Co.—a Connecticut-based manufacturer—and others; in return, offering unfriendly takeover bids. Other activities that had him slapped with a $62 million lawsuit included a series of stock and tax fraud.

Initially, a federal court sentenced Paul to four years' imprisonment, but in effect, he served 13 months. But let's step aside from that perspective.

Paul owned a robotics company and other notable investments that contributed to his wealth as well. This outstanding, but controversial, genius shared something in common with the rest of the family: shockingly high IQ levels. Because of this near-genius level of intelligence, it was not surprising that Dan's dad could pull off such a financial stunt with the US government, costing them about $8.6 million to collect just $3.7 million from Paul Bilzerian's total money. Unfortunately, even though Paul was being protective of his family, and even created offshore accounts, including a trust fund for Bilzerian Jr. himself, he hardly spent quality time with his family.

Most people have suggested that Dan got his wealth from his dad. Because of the infinite business trips and office duties, Paul Bilzerian—the Harvard Business School graduate — missed Dan and Adam's countless birthday parties and sporting activities.

You know what happens in this situation... the kids suffer. That wasn't any different with Dan Bilzerian and his younger brother, Adam Bilzerian. In Dan's words, *"Basically, I didn't get a ton of attention as a kid."*

Dan Bilzerian lived in a lonely world, even though he lived in a mega-mansion with stunning eleven bedrooms that could pass for half the size of Buckingham Palace, not to mention other mind-blowing features like an indoor basketball court, water slide, swimming pool, an imported volcanic rock mountain, and lake-front views. He lived in a Florida mansion, nicknamed the Taj Mahal, valued at 11 million dollars. And even though his father declared bankruptcy because of his FEC violations, they never moved out. Paul, a former juvenile delinquent, made life hectic and troubling for Dan—thanks to his bull-headed character.

An example of this was when he sued Dan's Little League Baseball team, the largest youth sports program in the world, and also a non-profit organization. Guess what? This lawsuit happened because of slander during an argument over Paul's $5,000 donation. Sometimes, some lawsuits can be petty; but, hey! A lawsuit is a lawsuit. They dropped this case.

And oddly enough, Paul only got to spend time with Danny when he drove him to school one fateful day, shortly after he had turned 10. On arriving at the gates, Bilzerian Jr. realized that something was amiss; this was further confirmed when his dad dropped the bombshell. Paul had been involved in several fraudulent financial deals and was to be imprisoned on nine accounts of stock and tax frauds

— a hard reality that dawned on Danny and set the pace for the life-changing experience that would ensue.

As expected, Dan's school mates started picking on him due to his father's predicament—not something one would love to experience. In response to this act, he would lash out and get into a series of brawls with his classmates. His relationship with them was severed. To top it all, he neglected his homework and opposed authority. In just a year, they expelled Danny from two schools.

With no other option, they enrolled him in a military academy with drill instructors overseeing his activities. This didn't last long as well, as they had to move over 2,000 miles northwest—Utah, to be precise. (This was where Paul Bilzerian bought a new software company known as Cimetrix and became the president).

However, school life for Danny here was not favorable as well. As Bilzerian Sr. was engulfed in more litigation, Dan's highschool education reached the end of the line when he brought an M16 machine rifle (owned by his father who fought in the Vietnam war) to school. In his words, *"I was so proud of the damn thing, I was showing everybody."* However, contrary to his expectations (and even though he had no intention of using it), the school and the authorities didn't take this matter lightly as he was not just expelled, but was also kicked out of Utah and told never to come back. Unfortunately, Dan Bilzerian had to complete his senior year of education from home. This prevented him from walking with traditional cap and gown ceremonies for graduation.

In search of a place in life, he enlisted in the Navy; this offered a whole new experience quite different from the one he was used to. So how did this ex-Navy Seal trainee fare in the Navy SEAL Division? Let's find out in the next chapter.

CHAPTER 2

M oving on to the next phase of his life, Dan Bilzerian joined the Navy in 1999. A year after, he joined the Basic Underwater Demolition/SEAL training—actually; he attempted this twice with little success.

Dan was part of the class BUD/S 229, 238, and 293. The United States Navy Sea, Air, and Land (SEAL) Teams, known as the Navy SEALs, are presumably the best special operations forces recognized and respected by many across the globe. It is common for people, including veterans, to assume Dan Bilzerian to have no major accomplishments at this phase.

However, he had undergone the training **"twice"**. Just so you know, it is difficult getting enlisted into this elite division, let alone completing it; and I will show you a breakdown of what it is like on the inside.

When the US Navy Seals are mentioned, you find several heads turning and eyes popping; that's because only a handful of people become Navy SEALs, and here is why: To begin with, you would need to complete 79 sit-ups, 79 push-ups, 11 pull-ups, a 500-yard swim in 10 minutes 30 seconds, and a 1.5-mile run in 10 minutes 20 seconds. Many people would love to be associated with this special unit, but very few can meet up with this rigorous demand—and this is just to get in.

It gets worse from there. An individual would have to undergo Basic Underwater Demolition, Parachute Jump school, and SEAL Qualification Training that requires 24 weeks and takes place at the California-based Naval Special Warfare Training Centre.

Not to mention "Hell Week," you can imagine how brutal that sounds.

Hell Week is the defining event of BUD/S training. They hold it early on–in the 3rd week of First Phase–before the Navy makes an expensive investment in SEAL operational training. Hell Week comprises 5 1/2 days of cold, wet, brutally difficult operational training on fewer than four hours of sleep.

David Goggins describes "Hell Week" in his book: "You Can't Hurt Me." as five and a half days of hell. Where the enemy, the instructors, do everything in their power to break you. They try to break you mentally, physically, and emotionally.

They make it easy to quit during BUDS training. Any time during "Hell Week", a white shirt recruit can just ring the bell and take their helmet off and they are out of BUDs training. When a recruit finishes Hell Week, they get the honor of wearing a brown shirt instead of the white shirt before completing "Hell Week" under their training gear.

Not everyone would make that cut, regardless of the level of one's interest. However, the sets of training are worth it.

To become a US Navy SEAL gives a few men the bragging rights of being among the world's elite military warriors. They are a highly trained, powerful and meticulous organization. With tactical capabilities, which include counterterrorism (speaking of which they took down the infamous terrorist, Osama Bin Laden, in 2011), special reconnaissance, direct action warfare, and foreign internal defense.

These guys aren't one to mess with. This was the unit Dan Bilzerian belonged to. Hence, it would say that being part of this team was a tremendous experience for him. Despite not truly becoming a Navy SEAL, he completed the training on both occasions.

And it doesn't end there; successful candidates would still pass through a pre-deployment training lasting 18 months – you can imagine how brutal that sounds. Not everyone would make that cut, regardless of the level of one's interest. However, the sets of training are worth it.

Being part of this team was a tremendous experience for him. Despite not truly becoming a Navy SEAL, he completed the training on both occasions. Here are the words of Dan Bilzerian himself concerning this event:

"I did 510 days of SEAL training. I finished the whole program twice. I was two days from graduation. I did the whole thing, and I did the whole thing twice."

This accurately depicted the tenacity in Dan's ever-growing mind. However, here is how it began.

In class 229, it incapacitated Dan because of the compound stress fractures he had in his legs—this was shortly after he had completed the infamous "Hell Week". According to him, *"I was supposed to let my legs heal."*

He went on further, *"Because they didn't let my legs heal, when I went to Okinawa, I got off the boat and went into medical and I asked them to look at my legs."*

Dan Bilzerian had a dislike for the US Navy Seals training. Here are his words on that: *"I was so over the whole thing, like to me in my mind, okay I've liked... checked this box. You know, I did SEAL training. I finished this. To me, it was like okay, I climbed Mount Everest... you know? I've done what I came to do."*

And in this case, all Dan was after was the training, excluding the actual service (Interestingly, Dan Bilzerian got out of the Navy right as the Iraq war began). Because of his contempt for the military, Dan ran two miles to compound the injuries. *"I ran for like two miles and just destroyed them even more,"* in his conversation with Besinger. *"Just because I was just so sick of the fucking military."* His motive was to get out. Having made it through "Hell Week" with broken legs, which had been for like eight months, Dan's request was finally granted.

His fundamental problem with the US Navy SEALs centered on the way the "ship" handled the situation. Despite Dan's legs being in a pitiable state, they took him to sea, rather than being placed on limited duty. Even though they were going to have him withdrawn from service, his superiors were engaged in a never-ending process of paperwork.

During this elongated processing time, his legs had already healed, making him forward a request to come back on board—this time, in class 238. Recalling the conversation Dan Bilzerian had with his commanding officer, he wanted to give the Navy SEAL program another chance.

However, the others thought of him to be crazy, including his direct superior who found it stupid. *"Do you realize that we are gonna be paying you disability, and we are saying that you are disabled, and you want me to approve a request for you to go the hardest military training in the world,"* were the words of his commanding officer, who further said, *"Are you stupid? Do you need me to give you a psych discharge?... What's the matter with you?"*

According to Dan Bilzerian, he was so "brainwashed", that while he stood in front of his commanding officer, he failed to see the humor in it. Being back on the program, Dan made it with his class of 238 that he had just two days left to graduate, which he would have completed had it not been for the disagreement he had with one of his administrators. This altercation resulted from a safety violation on the firing range. He was then dropped back to the second phase of class 239.

One thing Dan maintains to date is the fact that he served in the United States Navy SEALs. Besides, he got out as an E-4 (Petty Officer Third Class). He earned some awards for his time in combat, like Good Conduct, National Defense, Expert Rifle, and Expert Pistol. In summary, Daniel Brandon Bilzerian served four years in the military.

For the record, most people still feel that he didn't serve in the military or he quitted (and this pisses Dan off most of the time). We cannot deny the fact that he completed the training program twice, which is a feat few can say they accomplish.

But it's clear that Dan has sour grapes with the Navy. His involvement in the SEAL program gets brought up in interviews all the time and commentators, podcast-ers and youtubers have speculated on it repeatedly. For many men, not getting The Navy SEAL Trident is a regret they live with their whole life. But something like 90% of candidates for Navy SEAL training either quit or flunk out.

So why did not Dan Bilzerian not make the cut? After researching this question, I have come to my conclusion. His last time through BUDS. He said he was "admin" dropped two days before graduation for minor safety infractions. I think this is true, but only because the SEALs did not want him. If they don't like you, they don't need a reason. In Dan's own words he was not a good team player. He hated his instructors and let them know it. He disliked his time in the military. D.B. later said in 2022 podcast that he never really wanted to be a SEAL. He wanted to get laid by hot girls by being able to brag about being a SEAL.

What most likely happened was that Dan Bilzerian passed all the necessary requirements to be a SEAL, but the instructors didn't think he had the character or leadership and self-sacrificing qualities to be a SEAL team member so they fished up an excuse to drop him. He is not the only one they have done this to.

This does not make Dan Bilzerian a bad person or a failure. Some say he was just a spoiled trust fund kid who couldn't hack it in the military, but I think it's more complicated than that. Dan's father, Paul Bilzerian, was a Vietnam Veteran. The military awarded Paul a Bronze Star for Heroic or meritorious achievement of service. It's most likely this example was a driving force in Dan's life and causing him to seek validation from his father.

Even if he was just a spoiled rich kid who was waiting to receive a trust fund around age 35, he enlisted in the Military and he attempted BUDS twice! This shows effort on his part. He wasn't just sitting on his ass. And I have one question for all the people who have criticized Dan for being a quitter or faker or trust fund kid. Have you served in the U.S. Military and attempted SEAL training even once? If so, bash away.

17

But I find a lot of his contempt for the military as whiny and petulant. I do not believe the exaggeration that he completed Hell Week with two broken legs, but he may have had stress fractures. The SEALS do not want injury prone team members either.

One thing remains, the experience he received from the program partly contributes to who he is today. As you go further into other aspects of Dan's life, there are unique lessons to learn.

CHAPTER 3

A lot of controversies surround Dan Bilzerian's wealth. However, I created this book partly to set the record straight. When you talk about celebrities with incomprehensible wealth, the Instagram model secures a top spot on the list. Also, Bilzerian's answer to this question is straightforward: Poker.

To clear the air, of controversies surrounding the trust fund Paul Bilzerian established for his sons. Dan Bilzerian admits owning a trust which he only accessed when he turned 30.

To begin with, he already had a foundation built on some portion of his father's wealth; this is part of the reason he made so much money. Unfortunately, this was the money his dad got via evasion of tax and fraudulent investment activities.

In his college days, Dan Bilzerian developed a strong interest in poker. In an interview with the Daily Dot in 2013, here were his words,

"I went broke after sophomore year, gambled away all my money, sold some guns, turned $750 into $10,000, flew to Vegas, turned ten thou into $187,000." Daily Mail described the 5 ft, 9 and a half inches tall former US Navy Seal trainee, using these words, "A poker champion worth $100 million." Ever since then, the internet has always shone a spotlight on him.

However, as I would point out, not all Dan's money came from poker. Ever heard of that proverb, "It takes money to make money"? Dan was ultra-wealthy because he had the money to begin with—lots of dirty cash.

According to records, he played a significant role in overseeing a vast network of companies, corporations, and other business entities that protected his father's assets from the government. To top it all, he was the designated beneficiary to the trusts created by Paul Bilzerian during the 90s; this was a period when his father was indebted to the feds to the tune of tens of millions of dollars.

On the other hand, in 1993, the Securities and Exchange Commission imposed a fine of $62 million on Paul for stock fraud. He could only pay back $3.7 million. Where did the rest go? How did he spend it? Remember, with an above-average IQ, Paul Bilzerian could easily pass for a genius. He is smart and knows how to play his cards right—something Dan inherited and showcased in his poker games and business ventures.

However, this story isn't one the barrel-chested Instagram celebrity has come to terms with, as he still declines to say much about the amount or the roles it played in setting his career in motion.

To Dan Bilzerian, poker was business, and he was down for it. This game was all about the strategies and numbers — the same similarities he shares with his father. In his words, "If you look at poker as a sport... baseball, then I'd be maybe a minor league or high school ballplayer. But I play with T-ballers. If you look at poker as a business, I'd say I'm fucking Bill Gates. I've won over 50 million dollars playing poker. Who the fuck else has done that?"

In reality, very few have achieved such a feat. Dan Bilzerian and his dad possessed similar business acumen. For Paul, a huge portion of his wealth came from pump-and-dump stock operations. With several effective strategies in place, he increased various companies' stocks and sold them off afterward, making a killing in the process. However, he ran out of luck and they convicted him of fraud in 1989 and placed him in federal prison for 13 months.

Being smart, Paul Bilzerian filed for bankruptcy in 1991. He already had assets in his family members' names, some of which the SEC weren't aware of. A couple of years later, the commission declared that Paul owed $62 million.

You could have guessed Paul's response was? If you said "No money!" you were right. This went on for two decades, with the SEC giving Paul Bilzerian a frantic chase, while the latter stayed more steps ahead of them. I would state that the elder Bilzerian was more than prepared for the worst-case scenario, which he eventually faced by declaring bankruptcy and ending up in Federal prison for refusing to admit his financial lies.

Deborah Meshulam was the district court-appointed SEC receiver. She offered no comments on the Commission's effort to recover its money. Another spokesperson associated with the SEC also declined to pass any comment, stating that they deemed the investigations private. During this cat-and-mouse game, Paul Bilzerian played a fast one on SEC. It's quite obvious that he wasn't broke after all. Most individuals do that to avoid payment.

Let's proceed. Remember, we talked about Bilzerian Jr. (Dan) being involved in a conglomerate of corporations and off-shore trusts, right? Great! Paul Bilzerian had transferred high-valued assets into these byzantine establishments to keep them out of the reach of his enemies—so he viewed the U.S. government to be.

They wrapped his assets in a complicated network of financial operations that the SEC could only scratch the surface, making the case a tough nut to crack. If you stumble on any of the endless SEC filings, you would find most of them being written in code because of their complexities.

Based on SEC filings, Bilzerian Sr. had created a robust trust for Dan and Adam, the latter being younger and an avid poker player as well. There was a higher chance that Paul Bilzerian was masking his assets, as a judge noted in 2001.

21

In 1997, it was brought to light that they valued the trust of his two children at about $11.96 million in stocks gained from Cimetrix—a company in which he had once been a president.

Dan Bilzerian owned half of these stocks. However, proving that Dan's trust fund was, in reality, the SEC's money is as controversial as the moon landing conspiracy. But we can't neglect the obvious. This was also the expression of a former five-term US congressman known as Brad Miller, a contributor to legislation associated with economic recovery. Here were his words in 2008 when the case had turned into a full-blown quagmire: *"Transfers of assets to family members for well less than their market value has, for centuries, been marked as 'badges of fraud'. When the guy who has all the assets is suddenly poor, but his wife and kids are suddenly rich and he says, 'I don't have a pot to pee in, but I have a very generous wife and sons who will keep me from sleeping under a bridge.'"*

So, do you think that Paul Bilzerian's wife and sons were his handlers? And what do you think of the companies and trusts he created? Were all these events staged to carry out his objectives?

Now, here is what happened afterward. Even though 30% of the trust set up by Paul Bilzerian eventually went to SEC, Dan Bilzerian was allowed to sell off part of his shares. Before that time, he had already purchased a house in Montana without even seeing it.

Therefore, it isn't hard to trace the source of Dan Bilzerian's wealth. Regardless of what people think about his wealth, one thing stands out: Dan Bilzerian strongly built on what he had and turned it into a multi-million-dollar empire. Building your way up the financial ladder isn't a piece of cake. Even the billionaires of our time put in significant efforts to ensure that their financial statuses are maintained, if not increased.

And sadly, we have heard stories of some billionaires losing it all, including the likes of Eike Batista who had $30 billion of personal wealth and was ranked the 8th richest person in the world, and the late Adolf Merckle, one of the richest entrepreneurs in Germany with a net worth of $12.8 billion. To be fair, developing and sustaining financial wealth is not an easy task. You would have to be wise about your financial decisions in the areas of investing, business creation, and the rest. It would be fair to say that Dan Bilzerian did well, despite his lifestyle, which most people find eccentric.

CHAPTER 4

D an Bilzerian has a net worth estimated to be around $200 million–a mind-blowing fortune he built from (you know it already) his trust fund and poker. We know not much about the former because he wouldn't divulge much information on such sensitive matters. Also, the latter is an area most professional poker players still find hard to believe. A lot of controversies surround this subject online.

Dan claims to have won a whopping 50 million in cash in 2014 from private poker games with billionaire gamblers. He claims his strategy was to be thought of as a rich trust-fund kid and get access to elite high stakes poker games where the buy in was as much as 2.5 million.

Some poker players view the King of Instagram as a big fish who would rather play poker with celebrities that have no clue about the game of poker than with professionals who play this game for a living.

Put Dan's claim in perspective with all-time winning Poker Player's statistics. Bryn Kenney ranks the highest with 56.5 million in lifetime cash winnings and, second, Justin Bonomo at 50 million, and then third is Daniel Negreanu at 42 million. Dan's all-time winnings would make him at least the second most winningest poker player if not the greatest.

Whichever way they spin it around, his trust or poker game were the foundation on which he built his multi-million-dollar empire.

Few poker-players have been able to sustain their wealth. For this, Dan is an exception and worth recognizing whether or not you see him as a poker player.

Let's pause for a second and rewind; remember I mentioned earlier that Dan considers poker to be a business? And may I mention that business is more about strategies than the money itself.

To be frank, it would suffice to say that ideas rule the world. Look through history, check out past great geniuses like Nikola Tesla, Isaac Newton, the Wright Brothers; and also, modern inventors (both alive and late) like Steve Jobs, Bill Gates, Mark Zuckerberg... and the list is endless. They all have one thing in common which sets the ball in motion: innovative ideas.

Also, check out those who had the money but had no ideas needed to sustain and expand wealth. How long did they last? Not too long, right? Exactly! So, if ideas rule the world, one might as well conclude that business is all about strategies, and this is what Dan Bilzerian considers poker to be.

Hence, irrespective of what professional poker players think of Dan Bilzerian, he has achieved something significant for himself in this aspect. Dan Bilzerian's view of poker was to be strategic bout who he played with.

Danny B's poker style was, in his own words was very aggressive. He claims he played very loose in those days. Rasing and bluffing a lot. By playing in a lot of hands, he would sometimes catch the outside straight or top pairs on the flop when his opponents would think he was bluffing.His strategy was to raise a lot and play a lot of pots with In the end, the aim is to make money, regardless of who he is playing poker with.

In 2022, Jordan Belfort asked Bilzerian how he would rank himself as a poker player 1-10. Dan replied, "I would have to say in my day when I was playing everyday I was a 9 or 10, but now with everyone's styles changing and me not playing as much, I am probably a 5."

If he was as great as he said he was, then I can relate to that statement because any craft or skill you develop, if someone does not use regularly, it will fade unless you keep your skills sharp.

He credited playing and watching his college friends play poker online, in the early days of online poker, as how he honed his skills so fast. "When you have so many screens and tables open at the same time, you compress the time frame (of learning) by seeing so many more hands, so many more flops and rivers," said Bilzerian.

In an interview with Graham Bensinger, Bilzerian said. "I don't want to be known as the best poker player. I didn't mind being known as some trust-fund kid. That helped me to get into really big games."

He boasts his largest one night winnings of 13 million in one night in a series of games

Let's go back to how it all began. Before 2007, Dan wasn't widely known in the world of professional poker, even though he had been neck-deep into this game with his brother, Adam. Dan's presence was first spotted in a Lake Tahoe Casino with a suitcase filled with money ($100,000); hence, earning the name of the "suitcase guy". According to him, it *"sounds right"*.

Most players aired their views about his wild playing techniques, one of which included Todd Witteles, a computer scientist turned professional poker player. The cash game player recounts his experience with Dan Bilzerian the next day—after the latter's first appearance at Harvey's Lake Tahoe. According to him, everyone was talking about the "suitcase guy" who had shown up to the 740-room hotel with $100,000 in used banknotes. Describing his first game with the barrel-chested Instagram celebrity to Poker News, here were Todd's words, *"He was not playing wild at all."*

Before we proceed further, let me take you back in time, just a little bit.

Dan Bilzerian picked up his poker game skills from his days at the University of Florida—this was where he enrolled to study business and criminology shortly after they discharged him from the Navy. Dan said his studies were funded by a $6,000-a-month disability allowance, which he earned as a veteran because of his injuries. However, he had gone broke by his second year. With no access to the assets created by his father, Paul Bilzerian, it forced him to sell his guns.

With a renewed near-laser-cutting focus, Bilzerian Jr. was back at the poker table in no time. Speaking of his initial losses, he stated this, *"You have to go broke to respect the money. And I had a style where I could make a lot of money if I had self-control."* Speaking further on his experience at the Florida-based institution, *"Some weeks I was making, like, $90,000. So, I'm looking at these professors, thinking, what am I doing here?"* Based on his account of the story, he had flipped his $750 left from liquidating his possessions into $10,000, an impressive achievement.

Having bought a one-way ticket, Dan Bilzerian was on his way to Las Vegas to make more money playing poker. Once there, he made $187,000 – another impressive venture. With enough money at his disposal, he went back to the university, more determined than ever to continue his studies (which he never finished). During this period, Dan Bilzerian also took his time to build his skills in various cash games.

One thing that makes cash games most sought after is their unlimited potential winnings. On the other hand, tournaments comprise fixed prizes, alongside fixed buy-ins. With the knowledge gathered from consistent poker games, he drew the attention of the high-stake professional players at 27.

These previous events bring us back to Dan's moment in the hotel bordering California and Nevada. Narrating the events to Poker News, Todd stated the following, *"In January 2007, I was at Harvey's Lake Tahoe on a skiing vacation. People talked about a 'suitcase guy' who had played the night before."* He went on further, *"They said he had $100,000 in a suitcase, and played very wild. I was hoping I could find him and talk him into playing limit hold'em with me for somewhat high limits (but not nosebleed)."* Finally, Dan Bilzerian showed up. However, no one knew who he was then, not even Todd. According to the professional poker player, *"I tried to ask him if he wanted to go play $100/$200 limits with me, and he declined."*

Dan Bilzerian had a different approach to the game of poker. He was more of the no-limits player. He even talks about being one of the pioneers of this game style most people play currently. During that time, this sounded straight out of a sci-fi movie – one not many people could get along with. Dan proposed the same amount to Todd, but this time with no limits, which the latter declined as he was no heads-up no-limit player. Plus, he had just $10,000 on him for that trip, compared to his opponent's staggering $100,000. In the end, they both settled for a $2/$5 no-limit game, which was kicked up to $5/$10 before Todd joined in.

According to Todd Witteles, Dan Bilzerian was not playing wild at all. It was a pretty tight/nitty game, which Bilzerian, in Todd's word, "bitched" about all through, but did nothing to change the game's atmosphere. Todd went on to state this, *"It's not like he was playing every hand while everyone else waited for aces. He was also folding almost every hand, and basically wanted everyone else to start playing loose first before he did."* According to Witteles, Dan Bilzerian was mad that he was being viewed to be a rich fish from which people could extract money. As you would expect, Dan ensured that the game stayed tight, after which he finally stood up and left. Several months after this incident, Todd spotted him in Bellagio and shortly after, discovered more about this poker player of Armenian descent. By then, Dan Bilzerian had further improved on his poker skills and was more known in this world. In Todd's words, *"I thought it was funny that the unknown 'suitcase guy' from early 2007 turned out to be so well known throughout poker and social media."*

There was another event as well that played out similarly to the previous one discussed. This time around, it revolved around a big tournament, and Adam, Dan's younger brother was present – this was the same person that renounced his U.S. citizenship and wrote a book on it. This event spotted Dan's first attempt to win a huge tournament. At the end of the competition, both siblings came up in 180th place with prize money of $36,000. *"I wanted to kill myself,"* these were his words to *All In* magazine.

Joe Cada secured first place, winning $8.5 million. Moving from there, Dan claimed on Twitter that he had won $10.8 million in 2013, in one night of poker. He also made another claim to have won $50 million all through the following year. Presently, he states that he no longer competes with professional poker players. Douglas Polk, an American former pro-aggressive poker player, has criticized Dan's style of play, referring to (in his words) uber-aggressive hands, which along with other factors resulted in bad playing. In Polk's words, Dan Bilzerian was simply "a fish in the water."

He also stated that Dan made several basic mistakes, among which include many missteps relating to "really simple, pre-flop decisions." With regards to the former United States Navy veteran's story on running a small bankroll in the day, Polk considers it to be total BS, as Dan Bilzerian had neither good fundamentals nor discipline. Does this imply that poker had nothing to do with Bilzerian's fortune as he consistently claims? One thing is certain, Dan Bilzerian has played with some of the highest stake pokers and has beaten some of the weakest players in those games. Another concern Polk had was the way Dan's wealth suddenly grew exponentially. In his words, *"The idea that his bankroll didn't, in some part, come from his family is just nuts."*

One thing sticks out here, Dan Bilzerian is not a big tournament guy and he no longer plays with the pros. On the other hand, Dan puts out poker players in tournaments. In his interview with Brian Pempus, a senior reporter for Card Player Magazine, he admitted not to sincerely enjoy the game anymore. *"If there is a tournament and I can take a piece of one of the best players in the world, I am just going to do just that (laughs). It makes more sense."* Being one of the first poker players to play loose-aggressive, Bilzerian has become more conservative over the years – one experience that counts for maturity. So, I believe that most of his poker critics out there should cut him some slack. After all, he also admitted in the same interview not to be as good as many professional poker players – of which some of them have ended up broke.

Dan's claim that he built his multi-million dollar fortune on poker winnings reminds me of Elizabeth Holmes. The convicted fraud who convinced investors to believe her story and put billions of dollars into a lie. I'm not saying Dan Bilzerian is a fraud or that he cheated anyone. But people love a good story. People want to believe that a guy can come from nothing and be worth 200 million dollars snow balling poker winnings. It could happen, but there is no way to verify or disprove this claim.

One thing that is not desputed is Dan Bilzerian's love for the game of poker. He organized a celebrity poker tournament in 2015 which reportedly gave away $100,000 to charity.

You can watch a youtube video from January of 2017 of a live twitch streams, as he played online poker and Bilzerian just does not appear that sharp at the game. Just search Youtube for: Dan Bilzerian plays poker- Stream on Twitch. But that confirms what Dan already said about his level of playing now it's a 5 out of 10.

Chapter 5

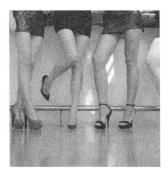

D an has apparently cracked the code to attracting women. You could say his philosophy about getting the ladies is: **If you build it, they will come.** Or build the right "Set up" and you will cum.

It's no secret that Bilzerian is a player and known to be a playboy. He has surrounded himself with lingerie and swimsuit models and porn stars. Has he used his money to get attractive women? Hell yes he has!

Social proof is a key to his success on Instagram and with women. Check out his Instagram account that currently has 32.7 million followers. Most of them are young men. Dan Bilzerian has more pictures of women in g-strings than Victoria Secret or Playboy.

Social proof is a psychological and social phenomenon where people copy the actions of others' behavior in a situation. Women are obviously creatures attracted to social proof. It's the case where if everyone else appears to love something, then you feel you should, too.

Jordan Belfort asked him, "What would advise would you give a man with 10 million dollars in using this strategy?"

"Easy," said Dan. "I thought you were going to ask me what a broke guy should do. If you had 10 million dollars. You should hire a hot girl for $120,000 a year to be your wingman when you go out. Have her talk you up and act jealous of you."

By the way, have you ever noticed when you have a girlfriend, other women seem to be more interested in you? When you are alone, women seem less interested? That is a form of social proof. It's a sales and marketing technique used repeatedly. Testimonials and reviews are big in sales.

Belfort asked Bilzerian in the same 2021 interview, what would you do if you only had $100,000 and he responded by saying, "Buy the nicest car you can and make friends with the hottest girl you can be around her."

Note from the author: In my personal dating life, I have found this technique profoundly helpful and used it before hearing it from Dan. Not the expensive car part, but by being friends with beautiful women. It offends most guys when they perceive they are being put in the friend zone by a hottie, but it can be a tremendous advantage.

First, because you will not hook up with and have sex with every woman that you are attracted to. Not even Dan can boast that. And this offense comes from getting one-itous, the belief that there is one woman for you. Being unattached to an outcome will get you results. Have fun with meeting people.

Second reason is that hot girls have hot girls as friends. If a woman is genuinely wanting to keep you in her friend circle and you can hang out in social settings, she will introduce you as a friend, and other women will see you as a high value person. Women do not want to be seen being friends with losers. If you can be nonchalant about this, it will boost your game. It is social proof.

Scarcity is the other tactic he uses a lot to attract women. That is a part of his setup.

His parties have had a ratio of 300 hot attractive females to 20 males. To paraphrase Dan, he has explained that most of the time, men give a hot girl so much attention, but when she is just one of many hot women, she has to work so much harder for attention. Men tend to be bad negotiators with women, giving them all the power. When a man tells a woman, she is so beautiful and that he desires her. He is saying he wants her, and all his cards are already on the table. She can negotiate for the best deal she can find.

But if women have to work for your attention, then you have the power.

Dan has boasted of having sex with 10,000 women and having orgies with multiple women, and having sex nine times in one night. I am not judging him or saying if it is right or wrong to be a womanizer. But Dan is definitely a womanizer. But how many other men would love to be in his position?

In an October 2021 podcast, Dan explained more about his mindset, behind why fucking a lot of hot women is important to him.

"It's kinda like this deep-seated feeling," said Dan Bilzerian. "That there's like a lack when I was growing up. I felt like I didn't get enough pussy and I always wanted more.Like in my mind. It's kinda like weed. Like–I obviously have enough money to buy weed. I got enough money to buy a $50 bag of weed–is not gonna bust me but I don't want to spill it, like I don't want any weed to fall on the floor. I will pick it up off the fucking carpet–you know, cause it's ingrained in me. And I think the sex thing also is like that. Or if I see a hot girl who wants to fuck me–I just feel like an obligation as a man to fuck her. I just do; even if I don't want to. It's in my mind, you fucking pussy, just get it done. What are you not going to fuck this girl?. I don't know? It's probably not healthy, but I just always had to do it."

Dan claims to have fucked nine girls in one day as his record, fucking nine full times in one day!

Does Bilzerian have an unfair advantage with women because of his money, fame and bodybuilding? Unfair, maybe not, but he has an advantage. He unashamedly went for what he wanted, a rockstar image and lots of attractive pussy.

While he claimed to be monogamous to one woman for two years while writing his book, he said in an interview with Jordan Belfort he could not see himself tied down to one woman when so many options were available to him.

One of the self-proclaimed things that made Dan Successful with ladies was honesty. He has claimed to be completely open and honest with women. He admitted to dating 50 women at the same time. In his terms, about 50 girls were on rotation but he said he would often keep a woman on a rotation of women he dated for a year.

What makes Dan Bilzerian stand out with the women, even though he is not the single richest dude out there, is his brand. A friend of mine asked me once years ago, "Would you rather be Bill Gates or Hugh Hefner?"

No one is idolizing Jeffrey Epstein for sex trafficking women. By the way, speaking of Bill Gates, Epstein and Gates were friends. Contrarily, Dan Bilzerian's ability to build a brand that attracts beautiful women and followers on Instagram is applaudable for the creative visionary alone.

Let me remind you that there are many good-looking, rich guys out there who don't get the same result as Bilzerian. So, what is the secret? How do you stop chasing after women and turn the situation around?

To begin with, you don't need 40 women or more around you to achieve success in this field. But if that is what you want, then go for it. However, one of the factors that make Dan Bilzerian successful with women is his lifestyle, which he has set up. Interestingly, it contributes to his brand.

In Bilzerian's interview with Larry King, he made the following statement, *"I kind of like figured out that life is more about set-up. You know, I wanna be like, set it up so that I can get laid without having a bunch of conversations and dates and whatnots. It's like if a hot girl goes to the bar, and she gets hit on 10 times, she can go home and sleep like a baby and not hook up with anybody. But, if she goes to the bar and nobody pays attention and nobody talks to her, then she almost like, hook up with somebody to feel validated a little bit."* He went on further with this, *"So, these are kinda situations where there's so many girls that nobody was hitting on and nobody was being aggressive and the girls would be like come to the guys. So, it's kind of like a setup thing."*

This is the mindset Dan Bilzerian is referring to. Yeah, money is great, but your brand oversees everything. Let me explain this further. Your lifestyle shouldn't be all about ladies taking from you without giving back; and I am not talking about sex. But, if that's your primary interest, then cool. However, what is important is that she adds value, not create a void in your heart. Many people may interpret this value in different ways.

Chasing women is the hardest and least effective way to get women. Instead, chase excellence and adventure and build a brand around your fun life. Women will come out of the woodwork to be a part of your adventure if it is exciting enough.

Dan has done this by throwing big parties, at the expense of his company no less, and by creating a fun life around things he loves to do. Things like collecting and shooting guns, traveling to exotic places, partying on boats, being into outdoor activities, enjoying gambling, being a THC enthusiast, having an exciting business brand. He has also helped build various attractive women's Instagram modeling careers.

Another point worth noting about Dan Bilzerian is the fact that he approaches ladies with indifference—and I am not talking about having a misogynist attitude. Before the fame, Dan Bilzerian had approached hundreds of women, regardless of where it was. Amid all these events, one thing stuck in his mind: The Law of Abundance. In a world of 7.8 billion people, 49.56% of them are women. When you do the math, that is about 3,865,680,000 women.

In the words of Dan Bilzerian, *"Don't chase and don't be afraid of rejection. You know... don't be afraid of rejection. Every time I see a hot girl, I'll just go up and talk to her. I didn't care if it was in the front of a grocery store... if it was in a library... like if I saw a girl that I find attractive, I'd just go talk to her."*

He goes on further to say this, *"I wouldn't go up and say, oh I think you are beautiful and all that cheesy bullshit. Have a conversation with her, see where it went, you know... At the end of the day, because I did that, it would just make me more comfortable talking to girls. And it was this kind of a numbers' game."*

There are two striking things about this. Dan never tried to compliment these ladies, and he didn't view them as being higher than him. Rather, he was just neutral and direct with his conversations. To him, *"If it works out cool, if not, cool as well."*

Most guys have this feeling of being insecure or inferior when around ladies. And this negative vibe is what some ladies feed on or see as a red flag. Once your brand is weak, then you are bound for a downward spiral. You can clearly understand this technique if you approach women a lot.

Let me ask you a question. How many ladies have you approached in the past week? Guys who don't approach many ladies assume that there are few ladies out there. To overcome the feeling of being a loser, you need to step out often with a high level of confidence.

Build a brand that speaks highly of your persona. You don't need to have all the money in the world to achieve this goal. By doing so, you would notice one thing—there are many women in the world. Even Morgan Freeman makes the same statement in his interview with Piers Morgan: *"Don't chase women."* This is certainly different from approaching them and striking a conversation.

In simpler terms, don't belittle your brand. Build a strong persona and they would chase you. Women love the chase. They feed on attention, even though this is one aspect they choose not to admit.

Who is Dan Bilzerian currently dating and who has he dated in the past? In July of 2020, Bilzerian was reportedly dating Instagram model Hailey Grice. Her birthday is November 5th 1998.

Hailey Grice

Hailey is from North Carolina, US. At the writing of this, she is 23 and Dan is over 41. It's unclear if the couple are still dating currently.

In 2018 Dan Allegedly was dating a fitness model named Hannah Palmer.

Palmer was born May 18th 1998. She grew up in Arizona, US. Her Instagram is full of bikini-clad pics, making her very popular.

Dan Bilzerian was dating Sofia Bevarly in 2017. He met her at a pool party. He boasted he had already had sex with three other girls that day but Sofia was something special.

Hannah Palmer

Bevarly has 1.8 million followers of her own on Instagram and an Only Fans page and endorsement with Bang energy drinks.

In 2018, Dan Bilzerian traveled to Armenia and allegedly dated Suelyn Medeiros. Suelyn was born May 14th 1986. She is Brazilian and a former Playboy model.

It's unclear for how long Bilzerian dated Medeiros or were they met. But the couple appeared in public together several times. Medeiros has a huge social media following of 4 million followers on Instagram and she has a very popular Only Fans page. The busty tan bikini model garners thousands of likes in her very appealing photos.

In 2020, she was alleged to be involved in a sex trafficking related crime with Peter Nygard, who (Peter Nygard) was charged with racketeering, sex trafficking.

Katie Bell met Dan in 2018 and was one of his girlfriends in 2018. She credits Bilzerian for her Instagram fame.

We can see Bell on many of Bilzerian's YouTube videos promoting his company's brand Ignite.

Dan had reportedly dated 37-year-old British-born model Lauren Blake in 2016

, In 2019 he dated 23-year-old LA model Desiree Schlotz

Lauren Blake

, and Cuban born model Leidy Amelia.

Desiree Scholtz

There are so many other women who were seen with Dan Bilzerian and assumed dating that we could go on for a while. The "Setup" as Dan calls it, works for him.

CHAPTER 6

Dan Bilzerian's Acting Career

D We can say very little of Dan Bilzerian's acting career, except Dan went to some length to attempt an acting career. My question is what makes a guy who has a successful poker career and has accumulated "FU-money" want to be an actor? My thought is that fame has always been important to Dan Bilzerian, even before he was dubbed the "King of Instagram" Dan had a burning desire to be famous. Maybe now he doesn't, but I doubt it. He wrote an autobiography entitled "The Set Up" and he stated he wanted to write a book after he read David Goggins' book *You Can't Hurt Me.* Goggins's book is a very motivating book and it is what has made Goggins a world-wide name and I can't help but think that is why he wrote the book, to be famous. Granted, he already was famous before he wrote his book.

Dan's Movie Career:

His first appearance in the movie industry was when he acted as a stunt person in a 2013 American action thriller, *Olympus Has Fallen*. In this movie, the 1.74-meter celebrity doubled for Gerhard Butler's stunts.

They also cast him in the 2014 movies, *The Other Woman* and *The Equalizer*, the latter being directed by Antoine Fuqua. In the movie, *The Other Woman*, Dan played the role of "Handsome Man at Bar". Other notable actors and actresses included David Thornton, Don Johnson, Alyshia Ochse, Cameron Diaz, Nicki Minaj, and the rest.

He played the character, Teddy's Guy #3 in *The Equalizer*, where he was killed by Robert McCall (Denzel Washington).

One movie stands out from the rest for a different reason. It was gathered that Dan had paid $1 million to get eight minutes of screen time, along with 80 words of dialogue in the movie, *Lone Survivor*, starring Mark Wahlberg. Contrary to his expectations, he had less than a minute of screen time and line.

Upset about this outcome, Dan sued the movie producers for $1.2 million—the initial loan amount and an extra 20% penalty. After having garnered much publicity and realized $1.5 million from investments based on the movie's commercial success, he dropped the lawsuit.

CHAPTER 7

M ost people's knowledge about Dan Bilzerian is limited to his flamboyant lifestyle on the internet, escapades, and squabbles with several women, and other trivial matters. On the surface, he seems to promote decadence, vanity, and recklessness, with the ability to do whatever, whenever, and however—to a certain extent, this seems to be the case. However, beneath the surface, Dan is a whole different person—a personality that has remained mysterious to many people, as he doesn't share much about his personal life on the internet. This venture capitalist has been building a business empire in the world of cannabis.

Even though Dan enjoys smoking weed occasionally, his interest extends towards the business aspect of it—creating a multi-million-dollar cannabis company known as Ignite. Before the establishment of this firm, Dan's net worth was about $100 million.

Currently, he is worth a little above $200 million. Here is a breakdown of his net worth over the years: $50 million in 2013, $100 million in 2014, $120 million in 2015, $150 million in 2016, $170 million in 2017, $180 million in 2018, and $200 million-plus in 2020. So how did his initial success in the THC industry all begin?

Initially, Dan wanted to start a marijuana dispensary with hot girls working it but shifted from that because it was so difficult to get the licensing and pass the regulatory process.

They founded Ignite in 2017, though Dan Bilzerian had been involved in using cannabis before that time. In actuality, his first experience with this drug was at 11, when he used a tin can. Throughout his years, he had been smoking weed. Then it hit him; why not go into the THC industry? That was when Bilzerian explored the cannabis world as an entrepreneur, rather than a user. In no time, he launched his company, Ignite, with the glitziest of launch shindigs in his Bel-Air mansion worth over $100 million. Full disclosure later revealed that Dan Bilzerian never owned the Bel-Air party Mansion, but his company rented it for $200,000 a month.

Interestingly, thousands of guests were in attendance to celebrate with Bilzerian and witness the exhibition of some of the company's wide range of THC products, including CBD oils, cannabis strains, concentrates, and vaporizer cartridges. His motive, he said, behind the establishment of Ignite, was to have smokers quit smoking and find a healthier alternative through CBD. Ignite is into the sales of CBD and THC products—the latter only being sold from dispensaries in all parts of California, which was a major pitfall for the company.

The company's CBD, Nicotine Vape, and Alcohol products are available worldwide, thanks to fewer regulations. Vape users can choose from a broad spectrum of CBD products, such as CBD oils, vapes, balms, edibles, and CBD pods. Ignite's marketing tactics bear similarities with that of Bilzerian's social media account, using bikini-clad ladies and CBD products. A lot of responses have been received from both fans and critics alike, with the latter accusing Dan of incorporating sexism into the THC industry.

The question on everyone's lips is this: how much is Ignite worth currently? It would interest you to know that Ignite generated $25.8

million selling shares valued at $1.50 in May 2019 – this was shortly after a reverse takeover of ALQ Gold. In that same month, there was a distribution deal between Ignite and Taylor Mammon & Nathan Limited, a UK-based white-label manufacturer. In regards to the deal, the privately held firm would be responsible for the manufacturing, packaging, and distribution of a broad range of high-quality Ignite-branded CBD products to designated wholesale and retail groups. In 2019 – just a month later – Ignite was listed on the Canadian Securities Exchange (CSE). You can find the company under the ticker BILZ. This event created a direct link to the Canadian market – a place where cannabis is widely and legally allowed and used. With this breakthrough, the company established an exclusive licensing deal with CX industries, an affiliate of Weed MD RX Inc., and a specialist in third product formulations. Under this agreement, CX is to extract, package, and distribute Ignite-branded products across Canada. In this aspect, the public thought that Dan Bilzerian had done an impressive job building a successful cannabis empire. His strength was in his lifestyle marketing; reaching a huge audience world-wide. Ignite offered one of the best cannabis and CBD products out there, and with their Canadian partners—CX industries.

Looking back at the company's net worth, the numbers don't lie. In the second quarter of 2019, Ignite made sales of C$2.1 million, equivalent to US$1.5 million, in CBD products. In six months of the same year, they had also made C$3.6 million. But in 2020, Ignite showed a whopping loss of 50 million dollars!

And Ignite was being sued by its former CEO, Curtis Heffernan, alleging Dan Bilzerian used the company as his personal piggy bank for partying. After the 50 million dollar loss for the company, it garnered a lot of press for the allegations. Dan spent $400,000 of the company's money on renting an enormous yacht loaded with 30 super models. In Dan's defence, he claims he spent $600,000 of his own money, besides the $400,000 the company spent on the yacht.

His accusers say that Ignite paid $26,000 to boost his Instagram following, and that Ignite paid for the entourage of models that followed him everywhere. They said Dan would just plaster the ignite logo on anything, guns, pools, bikinis and send the bill to the company.

But I ask, isn't that just branding? Dan even charged the company $25,000 for a ping-pong table and $40,000 for a rock-climbing wall.

"We are getting like super bowl ads for free," said Bilzerian, in a 2021 interview with Graham Bensinger. "The yacht was fucking branding. We had the goat skull (the Ignite Company logo) fucking front and center on a 300 foot yacht. And I think the Yacht rental was a million bucks and I want to say I paid for like Six hundred thousand-ish of my own money. I mean, on a 300 foot yacht with 30 fucking hot women on it, it was like life aspirational stuff. And that was the brand I was building, sort of lifestyle brand. And to me, that made a lot of fucking noise."

The failure of Ignite's losses in 2020, Dan explained, was because of the product not being accessible in most places and the black market being able to operate with impunity. The only areas Ignite could sell its THC products were California and Canada, but most of Dan Bilzerian's giant online following was outside of North America.

When asked by Bensinger if it was difficult to make the decision to pivot from Marijuana to Nicotine and Alcohol, Dan responded: "No, it was fucking easy." Bilzerian claims that Ignite will show profits with the new products that will overshadow the previous losses of 2020.

"Also, it's like one of those fucking things that people don't understand too much about business," said Bilzerian. "And they look at it like, Oh my god, the company lost 50 million dollars in a year, it's like Uber lost fucking 5 billion in a quarter. It's like some companies lose money. Most companies lose money in the beginning."

If you are an investor in the company, Ignite, the performance of the stock has not been good. It showed a peak stock price of $4 in October 2019 and in May 2022, it was trading at $.47. Maybe things are just about to turn around for the company but that it is unclear. It is traded under the ticker symbol BILZF on the OTC market.

CHAPTER 8

D an Bilzerian, the widely acclaimed Instagram influencer and playboy, has never been shy to show-off his mega fortunes. The King of Instagram, as he is popularly called, feeds the eyes of his 30 million-plus followers with some of the hottest looking vehicles in the world. Just so you know, Bilzerian has a car collection worth over $5 million. And it isn't just the prize that stands out, but the fact that these vehicles are actively being used, as opposed to having spacious garages filled with inactive luxury vehicles. Here are some of Dan's cars worth checking out.

1. 1965 AC Shelby Cobra 427

Dan's Shelby is worth $1.8 million, excluding the upgrades. In March 2011, an interesting event happened that centered on this vintage beauty. He had an auto betting race with his friend, Attorney Tom Goldstein. Dan was to race his Shelby Cobra against Tom's

2011 Ferrari 458 Italia, where the winner walked away with a cash prize of $400,000. This showdown was to take place at Las Vegas Motor Speedway and everyone was present to watch the quarter-mile race. In normal conditions, Tom's Ferrari was expected to beat the Shelby hands down. Surprisingly, Dan won the race. However, there are suspicions that his vehicle was a replica with a modern engine.

2. Mercedes-Benz Brabus G63 AMG 6x6

You will find it interesting that this monstrous ride was only available on the market for a couple of years before it was discontinued for a peculiar reason: to offer exclusivity. The $1.5 million SUV has been seen in a myriad of Bilzerian's IG photo sessions, both solitarily and with a cluster of gorgeous ladies. This beast packs a 5.5-liter bi-turbo V8 gasoline engine that produces an insane power of 544 hp and a peak torque of 760 NM. It accelerates from zero to 60 in just 7.8 seconds – pretty impressive if you ask me.

3. Rolls Royce Ghost

What is a car collection without a Rolls Royce? And for Bilzerian, this is not an exemption. This British full-size luxury car is worth about $250,000 (base price). Trust me, you won't catch the Instagram sensation riding in a base model. His white Rolls Royce, designed to match his Gulfstream private jet, is powered by a 6.6-liter V12 petrol engine and packs a maximum power of 603 hp. With such features, you can achieve a top speed of 150 mph.

4. Lamborghini Aventador

Another pricey vehicle on every wealthy person's list of car collection is the Lamborghini – be it the Sesto Elemento, Centenario, Sián, Huracán, Urus, and of course, the Aventador. With no more space in his garage, Bilzerian put his white Lambo up, with a licensed plate that reads "Mr. Goat", for sale on eBay with a starting bid of $400,000. Having upgraded the horsepower to 800, he sold the vehicle to DJ Pauly D from the MTV's reality show Jersey Shore.

5. Bentley Continental Flying Spur

Instagram users first became aware of Bilzerian's newly acquired Bentley in March 2014. In his post, he captioned this: "Somehow between my board meetings, I found the time to buy a new car." The

Flying Spur has a 6.0-liter W12 engine and generates 600 hp and an insane amount of torque. It also features a top speed of 200 mph.

6. Eleanor Mustang

The GT500 Shelby Mustang, Eleanor is one ride of a kind. This iconic model graced the movie *Gone In 60 Seconds*, starring Nicholas Cage. It has a V8 engine and produces 430 hp (for the base model), and either 600 hp or 750 hp for the supercharged version.

7. Other Cars

Dan Bilzerian has other notable rides in his collection. They include a Range Rover, a 1970 Toyota Land Cruiser which he drives with to the beach, Jimco Buggy, Polaris RZR 900, Can-Am Maverick 1000R, Dodge Ram 3500, Can-Am Maverick Max X RS, M35 Cargo Truck, Ferrari Superfast, Ferrari California, Ferrari F430, NASCAR, and a Fisker Karma.

Dan Bilzerian also owns a 1997 Gulfstream IV jet which he showcased to his millions of followers on Instagram. Following the picture which he posted on this social platform was a caption that read the following: "I told my Dad I bought this G4. He said: Congratulations son, by your age I had three." His customized jet has its tail painted with the iconic headshot of his pet goat, known as Zeus. It is quite impressive how Bilzerian grows, sustains, and showcases his wealth. Not many people can achieve such a benchmark.

CHAPTER 9

S ince 2014, Dan Bilzerian has been such a public figure. It's hard to separate his public life and his personal life. They have captured some of his life events on TMZ and on social media viral videos, these are some of the highlights reels.

The Las Vegas Mass Shooting

It isn't uncommon to find Dan Bilzerian in the news as myriad activities surround his personality. An example is the Paddock-Las Vegas mass shooting that took place on October 1, 2017. Dan was among those who witnessed one of the most brutal and devastating mass shootings in American history. The 64-year-old shooter who was spotted on the 32nd floor of the Mandalay Bay Hotel rained bullets on an audience of 22,000 attendees of a country music festival. He had several video clips from the event, which he shared on his Instagram account. The video showed him running away from the scene for safety. However, we heard in the second video uploaded, him saying,

"Had to go grab a gun. I'm fucking headed back," which he later abandoned. To the amazement of most viewers, we saw him in the third video heading home, saying, *"I don't think there's much I can do."* This created a lot of mixed reactions from online users.

In one of the videos, he described seeing a woman get shot in the head, with her skull wide open, unveiling a part of her brain. Dan wore a depressing look all through the footage, as anyone who in such a terrific situation would have. 59 victims lost their lives to Paddock and over 500 people had various degrees of injury. However, the Instagram king/playboy escaped the terror-stricken event unscathed.

The Miami Nightclub Brawl

A brawl took placed in August 2014, in Miami, which witnessed Dan reportedly kicking Vanessa Castano in the face. The model sued him over the face kick. In Bilzerian's defense, he stated that his female companion was attacked by Castano and another lady. However, this contradicted Castono's testimony, as she stated, *"There were two girls standing next to me at the table that were fighting. People started getting shoved, and I tried to separate them. Then Dan pushed me off the banquette, and once I fell, he kicked me in the face."* Having sustained injuries from the brawl, she went on to file a lawsuit against the professional poker and gun enthusiast. She requested for a settlement of $1 million, stating that more punitive damages could occur should the suit go to trial.

Porn Actress Janice Griffith's Lawsuit Against Dan Bilzerian

They slapped Dan with a lawsuit in December, the same year the Miami incident occurred. This time around, it was with the pornographic actress Janice Griffith. Part of the photoshoot for **Hustler**, a monthly porn magazine founded by Larry Flynt, involved Dan throwing the naked porn actress off a roof. However, things went sideways when she fell wrongly and hit the pool's edge, breaking her foot in the process. Janice requested a sum of $85,000 from Dan, which he declined twice. The 18-year-old at the time then filed a lawsuit against Dan Bilzerian and Hustler.

There is video footage of this event, it's obvious to most that he didn't throw her off the roof with any malice and that the act was staged for the camera but everything went wrong when Griffith grabbed Dan shirt and caused her to hit the concrete ledge of the pool. But Dan later admitted that the negative press of this event on TMZ and other tabloid news outlets actually boosted his following on social media, getting him more views than positive press.

"It wasn't like we were saying fuck this bitch, we are gonna throw her off the roof... We had been jumping off the roof into the pool for fun all the time. That's why she wanted to be thrown into the pool." said Dan. "I looked at it as something fun, not disresepctful."

The Bomb-Making Charges

It seems like 2014 (especially the month of December) was quite a rough year to the former U.S veteran, as he faced a series of legal battles. During this period, they arrested him at the Los Angeles International Airport based on bomb-making charges, which were dropped the same day as the authorities released him the next day. The charge thus read, *"Bilzerian has been charged with violating a law making it a crime to possess an explosive or incendiary with the intent to manufacture it."* It turned out to be that the actual charges centered around a fugitive warrant from Nevada (based on the report filed by the LA Police Department's Pacific Division). Despite his release, he was to be arraigned in January 2015 in Clark County, Nevada. The claim against him stated that he had aluminum powder, ammonium, and ammonium nitrate mix, which combined would make TNT. In February 2015, he pleaded no contest and paid $17,231.50 in fine.

Real Estate

In the last decade, Bel Air, Hollywood Hills, and Las Vegas has been home to Dan's many real estate properties. He officially occupies an exquisite four-story Bel Air mansion. The Instagram king reportedly rented the 31,000 square feet mansion furnished with 12 bedrooms and 25 baths for $200,000 per month—an increase from the previous $39,000-a-month mansion he rented in the Hollywood Hills. The new mansion spots a movie theatre, a wine cellar, a sports room, a two-lane bowling alley, and five bars. His primary residence is situated in Las Vegas for tax purposes. Dan Bilzerian purchased a 5-bedroom apartment in Summerlin South for $4.1 million, which he later sold in 2017 for $5.1 million. He then moved on to purchase a new property for $10 million.

Dan Bilzerian's Quest For Presidency

It would suffice to state that Donald J. Trump has paved the way for many celebrities aspiring to become the president of the United States. It's now a common belief that anything is possible. Celebrities like Mark Cuban, Oprah Winfrey, Dwayne Johnson (The Rock), and Kanye West at some points have voiced their interest in running for the presidency. And Dan Bilzerian is no exception on this list as he has shows interests in the White House. His first attempt was in June 2015, when he announced his bid for the 2016 presidency. However, it came to an end in December 2015. To the surprise of many, Bilzerian is ready to let go of all the women, drugs, booze and other frivolous and unedifying activities to become the next president. The Instagram influencer made his intentions known to TMZ. Do we expect to see him as one of the presidential candidates come 2024? Anything is possible. Besides, wouldn't it be nice to see Smushball, Dan Bilzerian's cat, in the Oval office? Let's look at his campaign promises for the presidential election:

Dan Bilzerian has promised to let go of drugs, alcohol, and sex during his 2024 presidential race and when he is elected. Sounds hilarious, but he is quite serious about it. We all would like to see that happen – and I meant his abstinence from drugs, booze, and women. However, that seems far-fetched to almost everyone as Dan's life has mostly been centered on these areas. When TMZ requested his opinion about how Kanye would fair in the 2024 presidential election, he replied, *"Better than Hillary Clinton."* He also stated that Trump would probably endorse Kanye. What are your thoughts on this? Chances are that Dan Bilzerian, being pro-gun, would join the presidential race as a republican. Apart from being a gun enthusiast, Dan supports the pro-choice and LGBT movements. He intends to set some things straight before taking a shot at the presidency. *"I gotta make this multi-billion-dollar business, focus on helping other people out, more philanthropy stuff. Then, I think I've got a good chance."* He stated in an interview with London Real. What business was he referring to? You guess right – Ignite, his multi-million dollar cannabis company.

Dan anticipates that this company would generate profits in billions soon. Here are his words on that, *"I should have billions of dollars by* that point, then basically just give the money back. I'd keep $500 million or something and then cap the amount that I could spend. Basically, I would be uncorruptible. That would be the premise of my running." When questioned about his motivation of becoming the president of the United States, he stated, "Just because it would be the last kind of box that I'd wanna check. I feel like I could do it. I feel like I did it for pure reasons. Like I really want to do the right thing, which I feel like is not usually the reason why most people get into politics." When asked about assuming the role of the United States' President, the former US Navy trainee stated, "I don't know if I would enjoy it. But I think I'd be one of the few people who could handle the responsibility and the power, and not get f*cked up with it. It seems like the last bucket list item." We all know that the US presidency exceeds just a bucket list. Nevertheless, Bilzerian Jr. isn't joking about this goal. He reiterated his motive during an interview with TroubledTV.

In his words, "I've got to make at least a billion or two billion dollars." However, he intends to give away the majority of his money before running for president. He went on to air his views about his political platform, "I'm gonna have a panel of people that are experts in all these fields, and I'm just gonna make decisions based on what I think is the right answer, not based on who's paying me or what company helped me get into office." He went on further to state, "I'll probably get assassinated." Interestingly, Bilzerian has a personal time with Donald Trump prior to the latter being elected President. Sharing his opinion about Trump, he said, "He seemed like one of the guys - typical guy - I'd meet at a country club or one of my Dad's buddies, or a thousand other guys I met. Seemed like a nice guy." He further shared his likeness for Trump by sharing a photo of both of them on Twitter which he captioned, "In an age of pussified political correctness, you have to respect the people who remained unfiltered @realDonaldTrump."

Dan Bilzerian's Social Media Activities

Dan Bilzerian is known to be an active social media personality. he highly engages millions of followers with his flamboyant lifestyle, ranging from hot ladies to all sorts of ammunition. Many influencers understand the importance of social media engagement. Dan is no stranger to providing the right content for his audience. He knows what they want and gives it to them. One of the unique experiences Bilzerian provided his fans with took place in 2015 when he partnered with Steve Aoki to host a mind-blowing party. 10 people stood a chance to access full accommodations and party with the two celebrities. There was a huge positive response from his audience, amounting to about 500,000 likes and over 200,000 comments. It points to the fact that Bilzerian had content, people wanted. His engagements are not limited to partying, as he creates other engaging tasks – some being charitable. Let's go back to 2013 when he created an initiative that centered on charity. Dan promised $100,000 to a family in need. At that time, he had about half-a-million followers on Twitter and 7.8 million followers on Instagram. You could already imagine the buzz the offer created as it went viral. Fortunately, a lucky family got the jackpot. There are other interesting giveaways Dan does from time to time, an example being his "fantasy sports challenge". On one occasion, he partnered with FanDuel to provide fans the opportunity to play poker with him on a weekend. The condition involved individuals picking the best lineup for the day. His engagement strategies are tied to his personality and brand, which he uses to keep his followers active.

Regardless of the negative impressions surrounding his ethics, we can't deny the amount of success Dan Bilzerian has gathered from his social media engagement. His 20 million followership bears testimony to how effective his strategies have been. Even though a large amount of his wealth and fame has their roots in poker, he has further augmented his brand through his social media accounts – most especially Instagram, earning him the title, "King of Instagram". As his brand evolves, Bilzerian maintains ever-growing followership. Besides, the party can't go on forever; hence, his shift in the brand at the age of 36 was needed. Nevertheless, his Instagram account still revolves around – you know it – money, women, guns, and breath-taking homes. Interestingly, his obscene qualities seem to have faded into oblivion as he has moved from being a party animal and cocaine addict to becoming a marijuana businessman and mentor – a step in the right direction. Once in a while, he comes up with hilarious posts to acknowledge his shared past. One thing remains; his following keeps increasing, irrespective of whatever content he posts.

Dan Bilzerian's Workout Routine

Dan Bilzerian is one of the few individuals that have stayed in shape, even with his lifestyle being classified by many to be versatile and hedonistic. A lot of people have always wondered what Dan's body-building routine has been like. In this section, you are about to learn a few things about his workout routine that would be of benefit. To begin with, Bilzerian's workout centers majorly on the chest, abs, and back. These areas account for Dan's strong build. Not much attention is given to the shoulders, arms, and legs as you can clearly see on his body frame. With his workout technique, you can build solid muscle. To achieve this, work on your chest and back twice a week. You can create a combination of mixed heavy-weight workouts with long rest periods and light-weight workouts with short rest periods. This routine aims to fully enhance muscle growth. You will need to achieve body balance by working on your arms and shoulders. So, how do you achieve this?

Your Monday workouts can contain the following: 3 sets RPT for barbell bench press, 3 sets RPT for incline DB Bench Press, rest-pause for cable rows, 3 sets RPT for incline DB curls, and rest-pause for bent over flyers. Wednesday workouts should include the following: 3 sets RPT for barbell squats, 1 set x 3-5 reps for deadlifts, 2 sets RPT for leg curls, and rest-pause for calf raises. Finally, Fridays should be more like this: 3 sets RPT for seated DB shoulder press, 3 sets RPT for weighted pull-ups, rest-pause for incline DB flyes, rest-pause for rope pushdowns, rest-pause for lateral raises. Just if you are wondering what RPT means, it stands for Reverse Pyramid Training. There are various articles out there that shed more light on these areas.

Some online users ripped Dan Bilzerian apart for skipping leg day. Everyone has workout preferences. In all honesty, Dan Bilzerian has achieved a great physique that rivals that of a professional fitness model. To begin with, he doesn't spend the whole day in the gym but still achieves outstanding body goals. He has a lot to achieve in the fitness world – no doubt. But, we can't overlook the fact that he puts in effort into staying fit always, despite his rigorous routines. "Nate, is it true that Dan Bilzerian is on steroids?" you may ask. There has been a lot of rumors surrounding the possibility of Bilzerian juicing up with the aid of steroids.

Dan had been quiet about his steroid use in the past. But now with his book "The Set Up," already published, he has been open about his use of steroids all across the spectrum. He even went to Mexico and bought steroids, used them there and with his buddies in the SEAL training, smuggled them across the border in their asses. Bilzerian has been open and honest, even in a self-deprecating way that makes him more relatable. On another podcast, he mentioned not being the personal development guy. But after having 2 heart attacks at or before 30, he seems to have slowed down on the juicing and has become more conservative, but he has definitely maintained his physique from his twenties.

Besides using performance-enhancing drugs, Bilzerian has been a proponent of getting your "T" levels checked. That's right, the good Ole testosterone levels. Danny B has been maximizing his physique with TRT for over 2 decades. Interestingly, Joe Rogan is another celeb that endorses using TRT. It's not a crazy idea to want to stay feeling young. The average male loses a lot of testosterone by 30 and may do nothing about it, making him weaker, and have a lower sex drive. There are a lot of TRT methods. Bilzerian and Rogan both recommend going to your doctor and getting your levels checked regularly and finding the right doses. While you can take supplements that help, nothing quiet works as well as direct testosterone injections. Bilzerian claims to keep his "T" Levels at 900. Another thing Bilzerian takes regularly is Cialis. Apart from the obvious sexual performance enhancements, it helps with workout performance as well.

Dan Bilzerian has the money, which makes it easy to purchase steroids confidentially. Additionally, he is known to be a heavy user of illegal substances – an example being cocaine. He enjoys partying all day long. Being in his early 30's and coupled with his wildlife, Dan stands to gain a lot from the use of steroids, one of which includes an increase in testosterone levels. His thick, insanely muscled waist may point to the notion that he uses enhancement drugs. Very few natural weight lifters have such a physique. However, we can't rule out the fact that Dan's thick and muscular waist is a result of his training and genetics. Besides, he has been bodybuilding for more than a decade; hence, his insane body structure. Body goals are not achieved overnight. In the meantime, he doesn't have fully trained shoulders and traps.

However, these areas can be enhanced by steroids. Having discussed these areas, it is difficult to find out whether Bilzerian is still on steroids or not. What is more important is that he has an impressive shape. It is clearly seen in his photos and videos that he has taken good care of his muscles, abs, and other areas. "How is he able to achieve that with his hard-partying lifestyle?" you may be thinking. Well, it will interest you to know that Dan has been a gym junkie for over a decade. It is possible to achieve insane muscle mass when you stay consistent with your workouts.

Point of fact, you don't have to be a gym rat, consume large amounts of protein diets now and then, or stay off alcohol to achieve Dan's body frame. You can achieve body goals while enjoying the things you love. All you need is to remain consistent with your workouts a few days a week and eat the right diets. Staying lean can be an uneasy feat, especially when many of us have varieties of 'substances' at our fingertips – we want to eat and drink what our body craves. Dan's healthy lifestyle can be attributed to his moderate diet routine. He treats food as a means of fuel to keep his body running all through the active part of the day. If you find it hard to keep up a healthy dietary plan, then intermittent fasting may help you achieve your goals. With Dan's ever-bubbling lifestyle, food poses fewer concerns. He certainly enjoys fancy meals. However, this bodybuilder isn't particular about what to eat, and what-not. For this reason, he doesn't keep a completely shredded physique. Once in a while, he develops body fat percentage increases. It would suffice that state that Dan maintains strict diets and workouts to look fit most times.

So how can Bilzerian take his physique a notch higher? First and foremost, he needs to work on his Adonis belt and waist, by lifting the former and slimming the latter. This would give him a Greek god physique. Most lifters tend to downplay their shoulders and focus more on their chests. By doing so, their chests overpower the shoulders. This problem stems from fitness coaches not being able to design the right training program that fully develops the shoulder. For Bilzerian, he just needs to get more involved with heavy overhead presses, incline presses, and high rep lateral raises. Furthermore, he needs to lay off exercises that increase the thickness of his waist, including deads, squats, and heavy-side workouts. Last but not the least, he can reduce his body fat by a few pounds, bringing his waist in by an inch and creating more definition at the lower abs.

Dan Bilzerian's Fitness Diet

It isn't uncommon for fitness newbies to assume that all they need for their body goals are constant body workouts. As much as physical exercises are great, your meals matter as well. You wouldn't want all your days of hard work to go to waste without backing it up with a healthy dietary plan. Even though Dan Bilzerian suffered a heart attack twice for going four days straight without rest, he still manages to maintain a healthy lifestyle by consuming the right meals. Here are his words, *"I have three full-time chefs who cook for me. I eat foods that are balanced, non-processed, high in protein, and low in saturated fat along with vegetables every three hours."* He went on further, *"Also, unless it's post-workout I have carbs that are low on the glycemic index too. I'm big on meat and fish."* Protein is very vital to the body system; this is a fact Dan is aware of. For this reason, he carries his protein shake along to the gym. *"I always have a protein shake as it's important to replenish glycogen after training. I think it's all comparable to what tastes good because protein is protein and I only have shakes after I work out."* He stated. *"If I'm on the go then I'll have a Muscle Milk and Nature Valley's Granola Bar. They've got good grains and oats and stuff like that. It's as good a meal as you can get when you're on the road because few protein bars are good for you."*

One thing that makes Dan Bilzerian stand out in the crowd is the fact that he lives by the rule "work hard, play hard". It is a ritual he finds himself devoted to. In terms of his workouts, here is what Bilzerian has to say, *"My whole life involves working out. So much so that one of my favorite quotes is from Henry Rollins' Iron and The Soul. 'The iron never lies to you. You can walk outside and listen to all kinds of talk,* *get told that you're a god or a total b*stard. The iron will always kick you the real deal. The iron is the great reference point, the all-knowing giver. Always there like a beacon in the pitch back. I have found the iron to be my greatest friend. It never freaks out on me, never runs. Friends may come and go. But 200lb is always 200lb."* These fascinating and compelling statements depict Dan's undying quest to stay fit. It also passes a strong message to every one of us that seeks to promote health and fitness. The next time you feel tired of hitting the gym or stick to a healthy meal, ask yourself this question: what would Dan Bilzerian do? (WWDBD)

Note from the author: I have found my "bio-hacking secret" and like Dan I agree that without a body that has low body fat and high muscle mass, you cannot really be a real alpha male. What has worked for me like no other thing and revived my workouts with high energy? For me burning fat for fuel using intermittent fasting and a low carb to keto diet. This one secret weapon has eliminated my beer gut and brought out my abs again, finally. And the ladies have let me know, too.

CHAPTER 10

M any people see Dan Bilzerian as the infamous playboy and jerk known to surround himself with loaded guns, objectify women, flash luxury belongings around, blow up his vehicle, and throw porn stars into pools. However, most of these people are oblivious to the fact that there is more to him than his eccentric nature. Having covered some major aspects of Bilzerian's lifestyle, if not more, some vital life lessons are worth noting. In his interview with London Real, he talks about pleasure, not equivalent to happiness. And this has partly been due to the lack of attention he received from his father as a child. We can all recall in the first chapter that his dad was hardly there for him, despite being born into a wealthy family.

Paul Bilzerian never cared for exotic cars, fast boats, expensive watches, and the likes. However, his neighbors did. Hence, as his son grew up, he got caught up in that lifestyle. Despite that, Dan has realized a lot about life—most of us do, as we grow up. In his words, *"The more the spotlight is on you, the more you don't want it."* He goes on further to state this, *"Just going out is such a problem... You need security. You know you're going to have to take a bunch of pictures and talk to people. And if you go out and you're fucking high, you don't wanna talk to a bunch of strangers, you know?"* Fame is great. But it becomes toxic when you abuse it. We all do get tired of doing certain things repeatedly over time, and this can be said about having too much attention on you. It limits your freedom. It's one thing to seek pleasure, and it's another to seek happiness; they are not the same. What is more important is that you do things that make you happy. So, I ask this question: how do you define happiness? How do you apply it to your everyday life? You may have everything that Bilzerian has, but still not feel complete.

I would say that the secret isn't far-fetched. Perchance, you may have stumbled on the solution in some parts of this book without realizing it. But for the sake of clarity, we will cover them again. To begin with, you need to rebrand your personality. This represents us as a person and creates an interface through which we interact with society. So, how do you want to appear? User-friendly? Or complicated? Remember, whatever you give is what you receive. This rule is not only applicable to people but also to goals and events. Taking a cue from Bilzerian's life, we find him to be far from perfect. Nevertheless, he lives the life he wants. How about you? Are you satisfied with your current state? Or would you like to take a bold step? It would also suffice to state that no one is without flaws, not even Dan Bilzerian's critics. But once your life is out in the open, there are no more secrets—this is Dan's everyday experience. Interestingly, he has a high number of fans and critics—everyone does. However, it is impressive how he has been able to handle the situation. Most people would collapse under the burden of having to deal with such a crazy lifestyle. As Dan grows older, he gathers more experience and gradually refines his flaws. Seeing the good side of him, he is one who is ever ready to become better at what he does. Success isn't achieved overnight, even if you are born with a silver spoon. Lots of effort is being put into ensuring that the result is achieved. If you strongly desire to achieve your dreams, then here are some steps to take:

- Decide what you want most in life and arrange your life in a way that it will make easiest to attain it. Most people would agree what Dan wanted most was to bang as many hot women as humanly possible.
- Work on yourself. As each day passes by, be a better version of yourself.
- Don't dwell on other people's opinions to the point that they affect your life.
- Rebrand your personality and stay in charge of your life.
- Do what makes you happy.
- Make each moment memorable. One day, you would want to look back at your life and recount those lovely moments.
- Never give up on your goals.
- Make a bucket list and start scratching things off.
- You don't have to be perfect to live your best life. Just be yourself.

Dan Bilzerian may not be the ideal role model for everyone. However, looking at his life beneath all that noise, he is one who is passionate about what he does and brings to life everything he touches. This factor is what truly matters in life.

Conclusion

The average person cruise through life without soaking in each precious moment. Most people in this category aren't even aware of the opportunities they miss while stuck to their daily monotonous routines. And there are others out there living their lives to the fullest. They live above situations and are in charge at all times. These are people that travel the world in luxury and style, enjoy the finest things in life, and live like every day was their last. In the end, they build so many lovely memories that make life worth living. Sometimes, they may take it to the edge. But hey! Come to think of it, life is just one. Every day presents opportunities for you to live life the best way you can. What matters is how you handle it. In the words of Robert Breault, an American operatic tenor, *"Enjoy the little things in life. For one day you may look back and realize they were the big things."*

How happy are you with your present situation? Do you spend time doing the things you love? Or are you forced to do them because there is no other way out? How determined are you to create an amazing life? Remember, there is a reward system in place for our present actions and inactions. Many of us have heard this saying "Live your best life". But how many of us act on that? You want to look back at your life and past achievements and be glad. You want every moment to be colorful and memorable. Nothing feels better than knowing you have everything you ever dreamt of. We all treasure that power to do whatever we want to, whenever we want to, without restrictions – whether we admit it or not. However, not everyone gets to wield this power. This is not to state that those in this reality don't have problems. Notwithstanding, they have built resilience to overcome them, over time—excluding the resources present to cater for these situations. One individual that strikes a chord when it pertains to living in the present moment or living life to the fullest is Dan Bilzerian.

According to Ralph Waldo Emerson, *"All life is an experiment. The more experiments you make the better."* Unfortunately, most people are rigid in their daily activities that they don't get to try out new things, meet new people, taste new meals, check out new places, learn new skills and strategies, and many more. They stick to the life they know, forgetting one of the key elements of life, known as **"Evolution"**. Life won't stay the same forever and those who chose not to go with the flow are left behind. As human beings, we need to explore the richness of life. You are not born to stay in your geographical location or get stuck at that meager-paying job forever. You need to constantly make a move. Be innovative and proactive. And I would state this again, learn to explore. This is one aspect of Dan Bilzerian's lifestyle that endears him to many people, irrespective of what others think of him. He doesn't give a damn – truth be told. He is living every moment of his life to the fullest and building long-lasting memories along the way. One of the things that make him special is the fact he can't be ignored by both fans and critics. Everyone has something to say about him. Besides, who said you can't live your best life and fulfill your dreams at the same time. Here's what to take home. In as much as you are driven to actualize your goals, let each moment count. In other words, make each moment as memorable as you can. Loosen up, life only gets as hard as you make it. Besides, you can't tell what you may discover by taking that bold step. Imagine how happy you would be at the end of the day if you spend more time doing the things you love. It's a refreshing feeling that would linger on for a long time. Our society is being choked and stressed out because almost everyone is uptight about one thing or the other. We have forgotten that we are temporary dwellers here, waiting for that faithful moment when we would take our last breath. Life is an adventure, but there are few adventurers. Speaking of adventures, nothing says it better than these inspiring quotes:

"One way to get the most out of life is to look upon it as an adventure." – William Feather.

"Quit hanging on to the handrails... Let go. Surrender. Go for the ride of your life. Do it every day." – Melody Beattie.

When you take a look at the internet personality and multi-millionaire, one thing stands out. He knows exactly how to let go and enjoy the moment, and this isn't just centered on him, but also those that cross his path. Hanging out with Dan Bilzerian would leave a long-lasting impression in your mind. He sure has a way to add color to everyone and everything. And for this reason, he has been able to build a large network of friends with the elites, including the likes of French Montana, Chris Brown, Travis Barker, Floyd Mayweather, Steve Aoki, Omarion, Jason Derulo, and many more. Interestingly, Bilzerian's finesse in branding extends beyond his personality. His company, Ignite, has gone through a roller-coaster of media attention at first boosting his reputation beyond leaps and bounds and dropping it down to lows.

As critics called Dan Bilzerian a fake, he has fought back to bring his company, Ignite, back to a profitability. Who knows what the future will hold. Despite the criticism Dan has faced from investors and conservative media outlets over his lifestyle, he has been able to increase the value of his company by 100%. With a large following of over 43 million active users on Facebook, Twitter, and Instagram combined, Ignite has been able to effectively promote their branded vapes and alcohol, increasing sales and profits. They have a unique approach to online marketing that sets them apart from other companies. With Bilzerian at the fore-front, Ignite will have plenty of media attention to come. Studying the life of this Instagram King may make you think it your life is so different from the crazy hedonistic lifestyle of Dan Bilzerian, but I want to leave you with another perspective.

"Failure is a mark of a life well lived," *Oathbringer by Brandon Sanderson.*

In a 2021, one of Bilzerian's biggest critics asked Dan what would he say his biggest regret in life was. This was his response:

"Man, that's hard to say. It's funny cause I said this before in other interviews, a lot of times like the things that you thought were going to be your biggest regrets are actually the things that have been best for you... I'm just saying like for instance, like when I got kicked out of SEAL training, that was like a fucking big blow. You know I spent a lot of time doing that. And I didn't graduate, and that was that. To me, it was really shitty. And it was like tough to deal with that. And it was like a monkey on my back for a while. But you know, like I said, other times, you know a lot of other classmates died. I would have missed poker at the right time. Like I wouldn't have gotten into poker when, you know, nobody knew how to fucking play. And I just you know, my whole life trajectory would have changed. I would have gone to college... later... towards the end of my UF stent, like the guys that were coming in were a lot more nerdy. the girls weren't as hot like GPAs went up and the college experience changed... So I just look at a lot of these things, and had any of it change I wouldn't ended up where I am right now. And I feel pretty good about where I'm at. So I have had, well, more than my fair share of fuck-ups. You know, probably learn more from my fuck-ups than my success."

"What's your biggest regret?" asked Polk again. "There's got be at least something that you regret? I know, I know—the meme is no regrets or whatever, but there's got to be one regret. Yeah?"

"Man, I, like I said, it's a weird thing. Because if you change one thing, you know you don't end up where you're at. You know, like I've been," Bilzerian stumbled over his words a bit. "I had regrets about my relationship with Jessica. But had that have, like, gone different directions? I wouldn't be where I am. And I feel like I feel like I've lived 10 lifetimes. And I feel like I've got a lot more coming down the pipe and ignite is doing really well right now. And I think I have a legitimate shot at becoming a billionaire within the next year or two and I'm excited about what I got coming up and I'm more happy with what I've done. I mean, I feel like I was like, checked most of the boxes that I wanted to check. So I don't know man. You know, like I said, I've had plenty of fuck-ups... I'm happy with where I am. So I wouldn't want to change it by altering stuff."

"I ask you for your biggest regret and you threw in there—I might be a billionaire next year," Laughed Polk.

This ability to reframe life events as empowering instead of disempowering is a key life lesson of Dan Bilzerian's we can learn. Jerry Clark once said that "Emotions are neither bad nor good but empowering or disempowering."

Emotional management is huge. We all have fuck-ups. Maybe some of us a little more and some a little less, but how we react emotionally is what matters. Do we let our fuck-ups take us out of the game for a day or week or a month or whole year or for the rest of our lives?

This life lesson goes back to the fact that you can't drive a car looking the whole time in the rearview mirror. Not obsessing about past losses is a sign of a winner while losers stay focused on their past defeats and mistakes.

I hope you have enjoyed this brief biography of Dan Bilzerian.

About the Author:

Connect with Nate on his blog at:
https://nateplissken.com/
and
Facebook
Instagram
Twitter

ALSO BY NATE PLISSKEN

The Surest Way to Wealth by Nate Plissken

The Coming Greater Depression by Nate Plissken

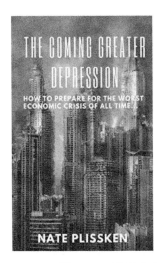

How to tell if she's into you? by Nate Plissken

Look for these books and more wherever good books are sold.

Printed in Great Britain
by Amazon

27702924R00046